I Paige Bridges

by Brady Thomas
illustrated by Randy Chewning

Harcourt
SCHOOL PUBLISHERS

Printed in China

ISBN 10: 0-15-351439-6
ISBN 13: 978-0-15-351439-5

Ordering Options
ISBN 10: 0-15-351213-X (Grade 3 Advanced Collection)
ISBN 13: 978-0-15-351213-1 (Grade 3 Advanced Collection)
ISBN 10: 0-15-358074-7 (package of 5)
ISBN 13: 978-0-15-358074-1 (package of 5)

4 5 6 7 8 9 10 0940 12 11 10 09

Paige could hardly contain her excitement as she and her dad drew closer to the school. She stared out the window, taking in the sight of the low brick building. Behind it were green, grassy fields. Cars crowded the parking lot.

"It looks just the way a school should," she thought.

"Are you ready?" asked Dad.

Paige nodded. "Absolutely!"

"Do you want me to go in with you?" he asked.

"No!" she replied. "I'll be just fine."

Paige's steps echoed as she hurried down the silent hallway. When she found her classroom, she paused outside the door and took a deep breath. "Act like you've done this before," she thought.

Paige opened the door and looked inside. Brightly colored art and posters hung on the classroom walls. The sunlight pouring through the windows made the room appear warm and pleasant. Students sat in rows of desks while a teacher wrote on the board.

"Please come in," said the teacher. "I'm Ms. Frances. Class, this is—"

"That's Paige Bridges!" someone shouted.

The whole class murmured as Paige felt her cheeks turn red. She knew people would recognize her, but she had hoped that she'd be able to blend in.

Paige's life hadn't been ordinary. When she was a year old, she had been cast as baby sister Sophie in a show that became one of TV's most popular comedies. She had grown up on the show, with her part getting bigger each year.

5

Paige made movies and videos, she modeled clothes, and she posed for a Paige doll. She signed autographs for loyal fans.

When the show ended after last season, her parents decided to take a break from Hollywood and moved to quiet Maple Hills. Paige had never attended school before. She had always had a tutor at the studio. While she had wanted to go to a regular school for years, now she felt uneasy.

Ms. Frances pointed out an empty seat. Paige felt embarrassed as everyone stared at her as she sat down at her desk.

The girl next to her pushed her math book closer. She pointed to the problem on the page, and Paige smiled gratefully.

"I'm Maddy," the girl whispered. "I have all of your videos."

Paige's heart sank. In her videos, she had played a pirate and the world's youngest astronaut. She hoped Maddy didn't expect her to be that exciting in real life.

When the bell rang at lunchtime, Paige worried that she would have to sit by herself. The class scattered, and she was left alone. Finally, she walked outside and sat on a bench by herself.

Then a group of girls approached her. They asked her questions about the show. They asked her about the actors and how she got to be so funny. They recited lines from their favorite episodes, and some even called her Sophie.

Paige tried to answer their questions, but she wanted to talk about other things. She hesitated when the girls asked her to say a famous line or to make a "Sophie face." However, she worried that they would leave if she didn't.

At first, everything was terrific. Paige talked about the show. She went to parties and signed autographs.

Most importantly, she acted like Sophie. Her character on the TV show was funny, and she always had a line that made everyone laugh. She was clumsy in a way that everyone thought was cute.

After a while, Paige began to feel unhappy. "I'm not like that. Sophie was funny because the writers on the show made her that way," Paige thought miserably.

She decided to stop trying to be Sophie. When people brought up the show, she talked about other things. She made certain she didn't dress or act like Sophie, and when people called her Sophie, she corrected them.

No one was mean to her. However, Paige noticed fewer classmates hanging around her. She wasn't invited to as many places or parties, and she didn't think the change was a coincidence.

"Maybe I made a huge mistake," she thought. "I was popular when I was Sophie."

One Saturday, Dad saw Paige sitting on the porch watching the cars go past.

"What's wrong?" Dad asked.

"Everyone wants me to be Sophie," she said. "I'm not Sophie, but when I try to be myself, no one is interested in me."

"That's because they don't know Paige yet," said Dad. "When they find out who Paige is, they'll definitely like you for yourself."

"I guess maybe I don't know who the real Paige is."

"Well," he said, "then we'll have to find out."

11

Paige joined a soccer team and didn't like it, but she loved the swim team. She also loved to draw and paint, and she shaped figures out of clay.

Almost without her realizing it, people began to talk to Paige about things other than the show. She found herself talking about the last swim meet, or about what they made in art class that day. She could discuss these things without trying to be funny or acting like Sophie.

She and a girl named Trina worked on a science fair project about frogs. They observed their frogs, recorded the sounds they made, and created charts with all their information. Their presentation won second place!

Early the next day, Paige heard noise coming from the house next door. A moving van was parked in the driveway. A boy stood on the steps, watching. Paige waved at him, and he slowly wandered over.

"Hi," he said. "I'm Christopher."

Paige looked at him carefully. Was it possible that he didn't recognize her?

"Where are you from?" she asked.

He sighed. "My parents are reporters, so we have lived all over the world. This is my first time living in the United States. What's your name? What do you like to do?"

"I'm Paige Bridges," she answered. "I'm a swimmer, and I also love to paint. I also just won second prize in our science fair."

Christopher smiled. "I'm glad to meet you, Paige."

"Me, too," said Paige.

Think Critically

1. How would you describe the town of Maple Hills?

2. How is Paige's personality different from Sophie's?

3. Why does Paige decide to try so many new activities?

4. What did you realize when the girls recited lines from Paige's TV show?

5. What do you think Paige means when she says she doesn't know who the "real Paige" is?

 **Social Studies**

Write a Paragraph Think of a famous person you would like to have come to your school. Write a paragraph about why you would like to meet this person.

School-Home Connection Paige is famous because she was funny on TV. Find a joke and practice telling it in a way that makes it really funny. Tell it to a family member.

Word Count: 1016